DISCOVER THROUGH CRAFT

ANCIENT GREECE

By Anita Ganeri

W
FRANKLIN WATTS
LONDON•SYDNEY

Franklin Watts
First published in Great Britain in 2016 by
The Watts Publishing Group

Series editor: Amy Pimperton
Series designer: Jeni Child
Crafts: Rita Storey
Craft photography: Tudor Photography
Picture researcher: Diana Morris

Picture credits:
AAACollection/Alamy: 20t. Ace Stock/Alamy: 16b. Album/Superstock: 7c.
Georgios Alexandris/Dreamstime: 26t. Barba1/Dreamstime: 27t. BlackMac/
Shutterstock: 26bl. brulove/Shutterstock: 26-27 bg, 28-29 bg. Nobby Clark/
ArenaPAL: 15l. cpaulfell/Shutterstock: 28b. C.M.Dixon/HIP/Topfoto: 27b.
Irina d'Elena/Shutterstock: 10bcl. Soru Epotok/Shutterstock: 10br. Alexandre
Fagundes De Fagundes/Dreamstime: front cover. Flik47/Shutterstock:
28t. Stephen Freake/Shutterstock: 26c. Gameover2012/istockphoto: 30.
Georgina198/Shutterstock: 10-11 bg, 12-13 bg. Aliaksei Hintau /Shutterstock:
24t. idiz/Shutterstock: 18-19 bg, 20-21 bg. Kamira/Shutterstock: 11b.
Kmiragaya/Dreamstime: 12b. Pidgorna Levenilia/Shutterstock: 26cl. Alieva
Liubov/Shutterstock: 10bc. Alex LMX/Shutterstock: 24b. Marsyas/CC Wikimedia
Commons: 8tr. Milosk50/Dreamstime: 6t. Tetiana Mishchanchuk/Shutterstock:
15r. Morphart/Shutterstock: 23t. Mr Pics/Shutterstock: 19b. Nella/Shutterstock:
14-15 bg, 16-17 bg. Nitr/Shutterstock: 10bl. G Dagli Orti/The Art Archive/
Alamy: 18. Orestis Panagiotou/EPA/Alamy: 16t. Nick Paviakis/Shutterstock:
10t. Photostella/Dreamstime: 20b. Marek Poplawski/Dreamstime: 22t. Prisma
Archivio/Alamy: 19t. Leon Rafael/Shutterstock: 22-23 bg, 24-25 bg. Roman
Rodinov/Dreamstime: 23b. Samot/Shutterstock: 1. Arsenis Spyros/Shutterstock:
6-7 bg, 8-9 bg. Piotr Tomiki/Dreamstime: 32. Universal Images Group
Superstock: 8cl. Anna Volkova/Shutterstock: 4. Haris Vythoulkas/Shutterstock:
12t. CC Wikimedia Commons: 11t, 26br. Witr/Dreamstime: 14t. Xiaoma/
Dreamstime: 5t. Vladimir Zuraviev/Dreamstime: 5b.

Every attempt has been made to clear copyright.
Should there be any inadvertent omission please apply
to the publisher for rectification.

HB ISBN: 978 1 4451 5077 2
PB ISBN: 978 1 4451 5078 9

Printed in China.

MIX
Paper from
responsible sources
FSC
www.fsc.org
FSC® C104740

Franklin Watts
An imprint of
Hachette Children's Group
Part of The Watts Publishing Group
Carmelite House
50 Victoria Embankment
London EC4Y 0DZ

An Hachette UK company
www.hachette.co.uk
www.franklinwatts.co.uk

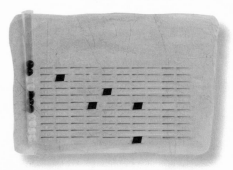

CONTENTS

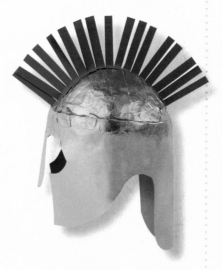

Words in **bold** can be found in the glossary on page 30.

Some of the projects in this book require scissors, a kitchen knife, paint, spray paint, glue, a craft knife and hot water. We would recommend that children are supervised by an adult when using these things.

WHO WERE THE ANCIENT GREEKS?

The ancient Greeks were people who lived in Greece from around 2,500 years ago. They were great thinkers, writers, politicians and scientists. The ancient Greek era ended around 146 BCE when Greece was conquered by the Romans.

Hellas

Greece is made up of a mainland and hundreds of islands. It is a mountainous country, making it difficult to farm. From around 1000 BCE, some Greeks left their homeland and set up **colonies** around the Mediterranean Sea.

The Greeks were also great traders, taking their culture and ideas with them wherever they went. They called themselves 'Hellenes' and their land 'Hellas'. The name 'Greeks' was given to them by the Romans.

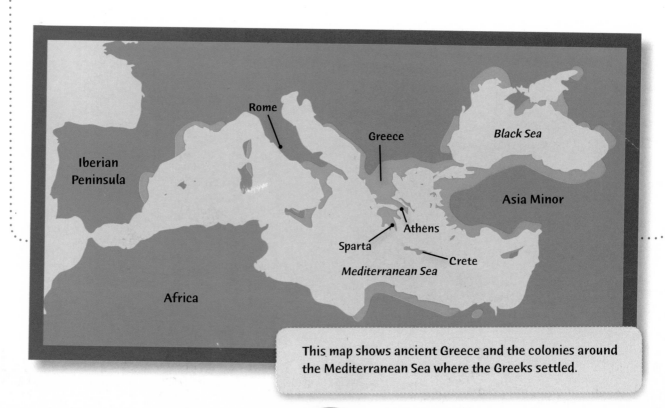

This map shows ancient Greece and the colonies around the Mediterranean Sea where the Greeks settled.

Early Greeks

The first great Greek **civilisation** grew up between 2200–1450 BCE on the island of Crete. It was called the Minoan civilisation after its ruler, King Minos. The Minoans grew rich from trade and built splendid cities and palaces, but these were later destroyed by earthquakes. After the Minoans came the Mycenaeans (1600–1100 BCE). They lived on mainland Greece and were great builders and warriors.

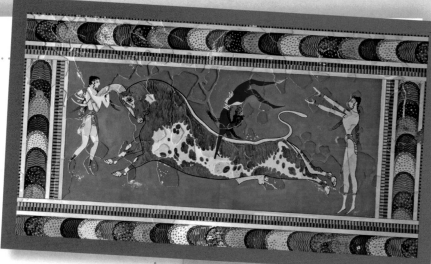

This wall painting is in the Palace of Knossos on Crete. Experts think it dates from the time of the Minoans.

QUIZ TIME!
Which famous **mythical** monster lived on Crete?
- **a.** Zombie
- **b.** Minotaur
- **c.** Yeti

Answer on page 32.

Classical Greece

From around 480 BCE, Greece entered a golden age that historians call 'Classical Greece'. During this time, the Greeks built beautiful temples, wrote plays, made scientific discoveries and established a new type of **government**. They also fought many great wars.

The ancient Greek Temple of Concordia was built on the island of Sicily in what is now Italy. The columns around the outside are typical of Classical Greek design.

Quick FACTS

- the Greeks called their country Hellas
- Greece is made up of a mainland and many small islands
- the Minoans were the first Greek civilisation and they lived on Crete
- culture flourished in Classical Greece

SOCIETY AND LAW

Ancient Greece was not one, single country. It was made up of small 'city-states', such as Athens, Sparta and Corinth. A city-state is the city and the area around it. Each city-state ruled itself and had its own government, laws and army.

The ancient Acropolis of Athens towers over modern Greece's capital city. The word 'acropolis' means 'highest city'.

Greek society

In Greek society, there were two main groups of people, free men and slaves. In the city-state of Athens, free men were divided into citizens (men born in Athens) and non-citizens (men born outside the city). Citizens were the most powerful and privileged group. Women did not have any rights in Greek society. Male and female slaves worked as servants or labourers, and had no legal rights. Some were **prisoners of war**; others were bought from slave traders.

Having a say

Many of the city-states were governed by groups of rich noblemen, called **aristocrats**. However, ordinary people began to resent how much power the aristocrats had and there were riots. In 508 BCE, a new system of rule was introduced in Athens. It was called democracy and gave every citizen a say in who governed them. Other city-states followed Athens' lead.

HAVE A GO
The governments of many modern countries, such as the UK and the USA, are democracies based on the ancient Greek system. Voters choose between **candidates** from different parties to represent them. Can you find out about other democratic countries? Which is the largest democracy in the world?

Deadly rivals

The most powerful city-states were Athens and Sparta. The two were deadly rivals and fought many wars. Athens was famous for democracy, **philosophy** and the arts, but life in Sparta was very different. The Spartans had a reputation as the toughest warriors in Greece and boys were sent away to army camps to train as soldiers from the age of seven.

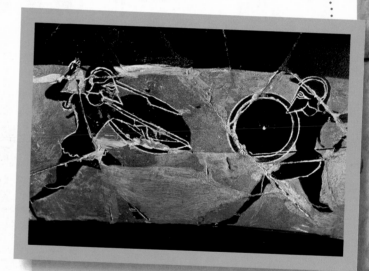

The decoration on this ancient Greek vase shows two Spartan boys training to fight.

QUIZ TIME!
What colour cloaks did the Spartans wear?

a. red   b. black   c. blue   Answer on page 32.

? What happened if you broke the law in ancient Greece? Turn the page to find out.

Trial by jury

There were no professional **judges** in ancient Greece. If you were charged with a crime you were tried by a **jury** of around 200 citizens. All male citizens over 30 years old were expected to volunteer for jury service. Each juror was given two **bronze** tokens to vote with – one for guilty, one for innocent. At the end of the trial, he handed his chosen token in.

These bronze voting tokens have either a solid or a hollow centre. Experts think hollow tokens were a vote for 'guilty'.

Ostracism

In Athens, unpopular politicians could be punished by being ostracised. Each year, the citizens wrote the names of these politicians on pieces of broken pottery, called *ostraka*. The pieces were sorted into piles, according to name. The politician with the most votes cast against him was banished from Athens for ten years. Today we still use the word 'ostracised' to mean 'someone who is left out or excluded from a group'.

These ostraka were found on the Acropolis of Athens (see p. 6). The names written on them are clear to see.

Quick *FACTS*

- ancient Greece was divided into independent city-states
- Athens and Sparta were the most powerful city-states
- democracy (government by the people) began in Athens
- people charged with crimes were tried by a jury made up of citizens

Make this

The ancient Greeks liked their systems to be fair. They invented a simple machine called a kleroterion that could randomly select jurors for a trial. This meant that the person on trial stood the best chance of being treated fairly.

Cut strips of card the same width as the slots. Write the name of a person in your class on each card – one for each class member. Put the cards in the slots. Place the marbles in a bag, draw them out one at a time and drop them down the tube. A black ball against the row with your named card in it means you have not been picked for the jury. A white ball means you have been picked!

1 Use a craft knife to cut the edges off a large sheet of foam board to give it uneven edges.

! Ask an adult to use the craft knife.

2 Use PVA glue to stick white tissue paper to the foam board so that it has a wrinkly texture. Use diluted brown paint to make your foam board look like stone.

3 When it is dry, cut ten rows of slots in the foam board. The distance between each row should be the same as the height of a marble.

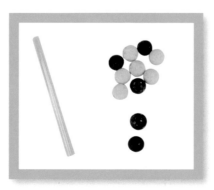

4 Cut a strip of acetate the same length as the short sides of your board. Roll it into a tube and tape it to your board as shown above, left. Paint half the marbles black and half the marbles white. Leave to dry.

DAILY LIFE

Most ancient Greeks were farmers, even though the hilly landscape and dry climate made farming difficult. They grew crops, such as grapes and olives. They also kept animals, such as sheep for their meat and milk.

The ancient Greeks grew olive trees for food and for olive oil. These traditional products are still produced in Greece today.

Greek food

The food eaten in ancient Greece was fairly simple. For breakfast, people often ate bread soaked in wine. Lunch might be bread, cheese and olives or figs. For dinner, there was usually porridge made with barley, or bread with vegetables, eggs and fish. Olive oil was widely used and was also sold. Only rich people could afford to eat meat, such as hare, venison (deer) and wild boar.

Figs

Olives

Bread

Hare

At home

Rich people lived in large houses, built around a central courtyard. From the courtyard, doors opened into different rooms. Stairs led to an upper storey. Houses had small windows with wooden shutters, which helped to keep the rooms cool. Inside, there were separate rooms for men and women, and quarters for the family's slaves.

This picture shows the inside of a typical ancient Greek home from around 400 BCE.

Greek fashion

The ancient Greeks wore plain clothes made from wool, linen or cotton. Men wore **tunics** fastened at the shoulders. Women wore a long dress called a *chiton*. Both wore cloaks draped over their shoulders – thicker for winter and thinner for summer. Some people wore leather sandals, but most went barefoot. Wide-brimmed hats were worn in the summer to protect people from the hot sun. Jewellery was popular – many pieces have been found in Greek tombs.

This amphora (vase) is decorated with two ancient Greek women, each wearing a chiton.

Quick FACTS

- most Greeks worked as farmers, growing crops and raising animals
- the Greeks grew olives and used them for eating and for making oil
- Greek houses were designed with small windows to stay cool in the hot climate
- clothing was plain and made of linen, wool or cotton

? What can pottery tell us about ancient Greek life? Turn the page to find out.

Grand designs

The Greeks were also great builders and sculptors. Although their homes were quite simple, their temples and other public buildings could be very grand. These were carefully designed to give a balanced look, and decorated with elegant stone columns and carvings, showing famous scenes from Greek myths and legends.

These columns are carved in the shape of standing female figures and are called caryatids. These are **replicas** – the originals are in the Acropolis Museum in Athens.

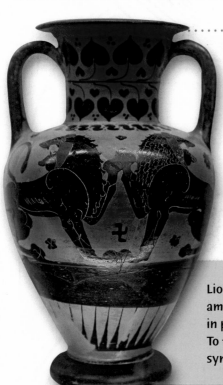

Lions – like the ones on this amphora – actually lived in parts of ancient Greece. To the Greeks they were a symbol of power and wealth.

Pots of life

Much of our information about ancient Greece comes from Greek pottery. Craftsmen often decorated their pots with patterns or with paintings of daily life. There were many different sizes, shapes and styles of pot, depending on what they were used for. An amphora, for example, was a two-handled pot with a narrow neck and wide body. It was used for storing wine or olive oil.

QUIZ TIME!
What was a *tholos*?
a. a Greek hat   **b. a Greek pot**   **c. a Greek building**   Answer on page 32.

Make this

The ancient Greeks were skilled potters and pottery was an everyday object for most people. Thousands of pots from this time have been found. Most were made using a potter's wheel and fired in **kilns**, which allowed potters to make pots in a huge range of shapes and sizes. Make your own Greek amphora using air-dry clay.

Use books or the Internet to find examples of ancient Greek patterns or pictures to decorate your amphora.

1 Roll some air-dry clay into a cylinder 10 cm long. Shape the ends into points as shown.

2 Cut off the points with a blunt kitchen knife.

3 Push a pencil into one end to make a hole. Flatten out the edges to make a neck and lip. Trim the edge with scissors into a neat circle.

4 Roll a ball and a sausage of clay. Cut the sausage in half and make two handle shapes. Flatten the ball of clay to make a base. Brush the clay pieces with a little water to stick them to the vase.

5 When the clay has dried, paint with terracotta paint and leave to dry. Use black paint or a black felt-tip pen to draw patterns on your amphora.

THEATRE AND SPORT

Going to the theatre and playing sport were very important to the ancient Greeks. Every town had a theatre where people flocked to watch the latest plays. Sport was not simply for fun – it was a way of keeping men fit for fighting.

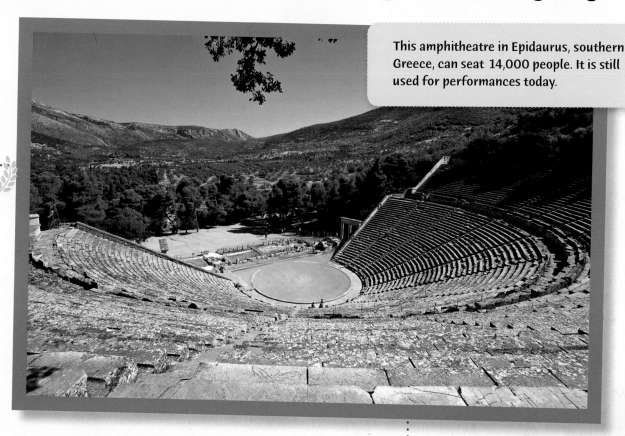

This amphitheatre in Epidaurus, southern Greece, can seat 14,000 people. It is still used for performances today.

Going to the theatre

Plays were performed in huge, open-air theatres called amphitheatres, which were built all over Greece. Some of these could seat up to 18,000 people. The audience sat in a semi-circle around the stage, which gave everyone a good view. The best seats were in the front row and were reserved for important citizens and visitors.

QUIZ TIME!
What did ancient Greek theatre-goers use as tickets?

   a. olive stones

   b. stone tokens

   c. silver coins

   Answer on page 32.

Comedies and tragedies

There were two main types of ancient Greek play – comedies and tragedies. Comedies were usually about ordinary people, with slapstick humour and jokes. Tragedies were often about the gods or heroes of the past. Both were extremely popular. Top Greek writers, such as Sophocles, Aristophanes and Aeschylus, became celebrities of the time.

Quick FACTS

- the largest Greek theatres could seat up to 18,000 people
- there were two main types of play – comedies and tragedies
- all ancient Greek actors were men – they played women's roles, too

This modern production of *The Oresteia* - a tragedy by playwright, Aeschylus - is performed by actors wearing masks, just as they would have done in ancient times.

Actors and acting

In ancient Greece, only men were allowed to become actors. They played every part, including women. Actors wore painted masks to show the type of character they were playing. To change character, an actor changed his mask. Because the theatres were so big, actors also wore padded costumes and large wigs so that the audience could see them from far away.

Carvings of actors' masks decorate the ancient Greek theatre at Myra, which today is in Turkey.

? What major sporting event did the ancient Greeks invent? Turn the page to find out.

Olympic Games

The biggest sporting event in ancient Greece was the Olympic Games. They were first held in Olympia in 776 BCE, in honour of the god, Zeus.

Athletes travelled from all over Greece to compete. A **truce** was called between the rival city-states so that people could travel in safety.

The main events

The main events in the ancient Olympics were: running, wrestling, boxing, horse racing, **chariot** racing and the pentathlon. Prizes were awarded on the last day of the games. Winners received a wreath of olive leaves and a hero's welcome back home.

This vase is decorated to show athletes competing in an Olympic Games wrestling competition.

It is a tradition to keep the Olympic Flame burning throughout the games. It **symbolises** the Greek god, Zeus, bringing fire to mankind.

HAVE A GO
At the ancient Olympics, the five pentathlon events were: running, wrestling, jumping, **discus** and javelin. It was designed to find the best all-round athlete. Can you find out about the pentathlon held at the Olympic Games today? Which events does the modern pentathlon include?

Make this

Olive trees were important to the ancient Greeks and they were a symbol of peace, wisdom and victory. Make lots of victory wreaths to crown the winners of each event at a school sports day.

Wreaths are found in many other cultures, especially in Europe. The Romans made theirs from laurel leaves. Wreaths made from wheat were made in ancient Greece and are still made in other European countries today. They are made to protect against poor harvests. Today, wreaths are often placed on coffins or **memorials** to remember people who have died.

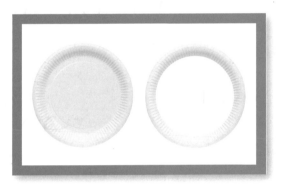

1 Carefully cut the centre out of a paper plate to make a ring.

2 Cut out lots of leaf shapes from dark-green and light-green card. Cut olive shapes from black paper.

3 Turn the ring over and glue the leaf shapes all around the ring, overlapping the leaves as shown.

4 Glue a few olives among the leaves around your wreath.

GREEKS IN BATTLE

Fighting often broke out between the city-states. From 431–404 BCE, Athens and Sparta fought the Peloponnesian War. At other times, the Greeks forgot their quarrels and joined forces against their main enemy – Persia.

Heroic hoplites

Greek foot soldiers were called hoplites. They made up the backbone of the army and were armed with long spears and large, round shields. They wore helmets made of bronze, sometimes with horsehair on top. In battle, hoplites lined up in ranks and locked their shields together. This was known as a phalanx. Once a phalanx started marching, it was very tough for enemy soldiers to break through.

This pot shows two lines of enemy hoplites. Each line has their shields locked together.

This mound is where 192 Athenians, who died at the Battle of Marathon in 490 BCE, are buried.

Persian Wars

In 490 BCE, the Persians (from modern-day Iran) invaded Greece. This began a series of wars that lasted until 449 BCE. One of the most famous battles was the Battle of Marathon. The Greeks were heavily outnumbered, but they won the battle. According to legend, a Greek soldier called Pheidippides ran from Marathon to Athens with news of the victory. This amazing feat was the inspiration for the modern marathon race, which is run over 42.195 km – the same distance Pheidippides ran.

Every year, runners take part in the London Marathon.

Quick FACTS

- hoplites were foot soldiers in the Greek army
- the ancient Greeks fought the Persians in the Persian Wars from 490–449 BCE
- the Greeks beat the Persians at the Battle of Marathon in 490 BCE

HAVE A GO

A hoplite's shield was decorated with a design (see p. 18). It was often a symbol of his city-state or family. These designs allowed hoplites to identify each other in the thick of battle. Try designing your own shield. You can research some images on the Internet or make up your own.

? Did the Greeks fight any battles at sea? Turn the page to find out.

War at sea

Greek warships were called triremes. They had sails and three rows of oars on each side. They probably carried around 200 men, including archers and soldiers. Fixed to the prow (front) was a sharp metal ram. In battle, the triremes rammed enemy ships in order to sink them.

One hundred and seventy rowers are needed to power the three rows of oars on the replica trireme, HN *Olympias*.

This monument on the island of Salamis is of Greek warriors fighting in the Battle of Salamis.

QUIZ TIME!

Why did triremes have an eye painted on the prow?

a. **to see where it is going**
b. **to tell the front from the back**
c. **to scare the enemy**

Answer on page 32.

Battle of Salamis

The greatest sea battle in ancient Greece took place in 480 BCE around the island of Salamis, off the coast of Athens. A huge fleet of about 500 Persian ships sailed into a narrow channel where the Greek navy took them by surprise. It was difficult for the Persians to manoeuvre their ships, and the Greeks attacked and sunk many of them.

Make this

Hoplite helmets were made of bronze to protect against blows from swords and spears. Many had a decorative brush made of horsehair – the thick, wiry hairs plucked from horses' manes and tails.

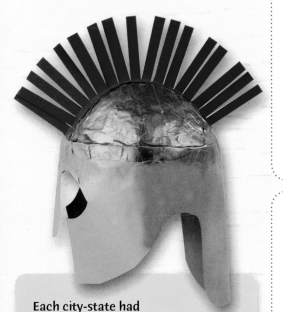

Each city-state had slightly different style of helmet. Research the differences between a Corinthian and a Thracian helmet.

1 Blow up a balloon and sit it in a bowl. Cover the top half with three layers of papier-mâché. When it is dry, remove the papier-mâché cap and trim the edges to neaten them.

2 Take a piece of card that is wider than your face and long enough to wrap around your head. Cut away areas for your eyes and mouth as shown. Tape this to the cap and cover all the joins with more layers of papier-mâché. Leave to dry and then paint it all gold.

3 Fold a piece of red card that is about 10 cm wide and 20 cm long in half. Bend up 1 cm of both of the unfolded long edges to create a base. Stick a piece of double-sided tape along the base.

4 Cut the red card into 1 cm strips. Peel off the protective strip from the double-sided tape and then stick each strip on top of your helmet as shown to create the horsehair brush effect.

WISDOM AND WRITING

The ancient Greeks were great thinkers, scientists, doctors, mathematicians and writers. At first, they thought that everything in life and nature was the work of the gods. Later, they began to make sense of the world in other ways.

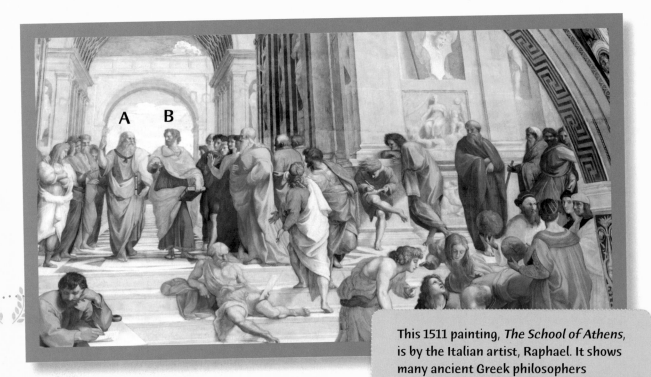

This 1511 painting, *The School of Athens*, is by the Italian artist, Raphael. It shows many ancient Greek philosophers including Plato (A) and Aristotle (B).

The search for knowledge

The ancient Greeks were the first philosophers, meaning 'lovers of knowledge'. They questioned the world around them and tried to answer difficult questions, such as 'what is the meaning of life?'. They also looked at how people should try to live and how countries should be governed. Some of the greatest Greek philosophers were Aristotle, Plato and Socrates. Their work is still studied today.

QUIZ TIME!
Where did the philosopher, Diogenes, live?

a. in a house
b. in a large pot
c. in a ship

Answer on page 32.

Science and maths

Some of the greatest scientists and mathematicians came from ancient Greece. One day, when he was sitting in the bath, the scientist Archimedes discovered an important law of physics. He noticed that the water overflowed. From this, he calculated that an object always **displaces** its own volume of water. This explains why things float or sink.

The Archimedes Screw is a simple machine invented by Archimedes that can move water from low ground to high ground.

Call the doctor

Ancient Greek doctors were among the first to study illnesses in a practical, scientific way. Before this, people prayed to the gods when they were sick. The most famous Greek doctor was Hippocrates. In his medical school on the island of Kos, he taught his students to examine patients carefully and try to work out what was causing them to be ill.

These are the ruins of an *asclepeion* ('healing temple') on the island of Kos, where it is thought Hippocrates studied and taught medicine.

? How did the Greeks write their ideas down? Turn the page to find out.

Greek alphabet

Greeks used an alphabet based on that of the Phoenicians, who were traders from the Middle East. The Phoenician alphabet only used consonants so the Greeks had to add vowels. At first, the Greeks wrote from right to left and then tried changing direction at the end of each line. Later, they settled on writing from left to right. Many Greek letters are still used as symbols in mathematics.

These Greek letters are carved into a stone tablet.

The Greek letter 'pi' is also a mathematical symbol for the relationship between a circle's **circumference** and its **diameter**.

Quick FACTS

• philosopher is a Greek word for a 'lover of knowledge'
• Aristotle, Plato and Socrates were great Greek philosophers
• legend says that Archimedes made his famous discovery in the bath
• modern doctors still follow some of Hippocrates' ideas today

HAVE A GO
Many of the words we use today come from ancient Greek words. For example, 'microscope' means 'to see things that are small'. 'Geography' means 'description of the Earth'. 'Alphabet' comes from the first two letters of the Greek alphabet – alpha and beta. Can you find out about any more?

Make this

The first scrolls were made by the ancient Egyptians. Greek scrolls would have been made of very thin animal skin, called parchment. When books were invented, scrolls were no longer used.

Instead of the alphabet you could write Greek words on your scroll. You could even write a story (in whatever language you like!) on your scroll. Read it aloud as you unroll your scroll.

! Be careful with hot water.

1 Tear thin strips off the edges of two sheets of A4 paper.

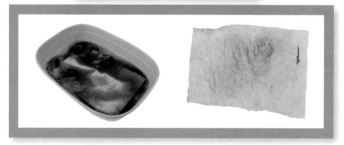

2 Put five teabags in a large plastic tray and pour hot water on them. Put the paper in the water for 5 minutes. Drain off the water and leave the paper to dry. Be careful with it because it is fragile at this stage.

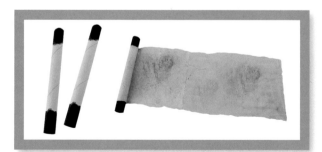

3 Paint the edges of two cardboard tubes brown. Leave to dry. Tape the short edges of the sheets together and tape a tube to each end of the paper.

4 Write the Greek alphabet, on the paper. Roll up your scroll from both ends. Unroll it to read your scroll.

RELIGION, GODS AND GODDESSES

The ancient Greeks believed in many gods and goddesses who watched over them and controlled events in the world. Gods and goddesses were believed to be powerful and immortal.

Mount Olympus is the highest mountain in Greece. It is 2,918 m tall at its highest point.

The Olympians

The Greeks believed that 12 of the most important gods and goddesses lived on Mount Olympus. Zeus was king of the gods, and god of the sky and thunder. He was married to Hera, goddess of women and marriage. Zeus's brothers were Poseidon, god of the sea, and Hades, god of the Underworld. Hades' three-headed dog, Cerberus, guarded the Underworld.

Zeus

Hera

Poseidon

Hades

Temples and shrines

The Greeks built beautiful temples to the gods and goddesses where they went to worship and make offerings. They might pray for help if they were sick, were about to go on a dangerous journey or were hoping for a good harvest. The Greeks also had shrines at home.

The Temple of Olympian Zeus in Athens was the largest of the Greek temples. Today only a few ruined columns remain.

Death and the Underworld

According to Greek beliefs, the souls of the dead went to the Underworld, an underground kingdom, ruled by Hades. To reach the Underworld, souls had to pay Charon, the ferryman, to take them across the River Styx. After this, three judges decided on their fate. If a person had lived a wicked life they were banished to Tartarus, a terrible pit of torture.

This pottery cup shows Charon steering his boat across the River Styx.

Quick FACTS

- Zeus was the king of the gods and the ruler of the heavens
- the 12 most important gods and goddesses lived on Mount Olympus
- the Greeks built temples as the gods' homes on Earth
- the Underworld was guarded by a three-headed dog called Cerberus

QUIZ TIME!

What did Charon take as payment to take souls over the River Styx?

a. a coin
b. a pot of olive oil
c. a sheep's bone

Answer on page 32.

? Which Greek hero killed a terrible monster? Turn the page to find out.

Mythical heroes

The Greeks told many stories, called myths, about their gods, goddesses and heroes. One myth tells of the hero, Perseus, and his daring journey to bring back the head of the **gorgon**, Medusa. Perseus braved many challenges and monsters to bring the head home in order to save his mother from marrying the evil king, Polydectes.

The myth says that Medusa's hair was made of snakes and that looking into her eyes would turn you to stone!

Roman rule

By 146 BCE, Greece had been conquered by the Romans. The Romans were greatly influenced by Greek ideas. They made copies of the best Greek sculptures, copied out hundreds of Greek manuscripts and took over many of the Greek gods as their own. In this way, they helped to keep Greek culture alive, long after the Greek age had come to an end.

The Greek god, Poseidon and the Roman god, Neptune both carry a three-pronged spear called a trident. Both are known as the god of the sea.

HAVE A GO
Read some more of the myths that the Greeks told about their gods. Then try writing a myth of your own. You can base it on an existing myth but make it more exciting by turning it into a cartoon strip, a blog or a diary, written in the god's voice.

Make this

The Greek god Hermes is known as a trickster and a messenger. He is often shown with winged sandals, which he used to take messages quickly back and forth. Make your own ankle wings to become a messenger of the gods!

Make two of these winged ribbons - one for each ankle. Wind the ribbon several times around each ankle to make sure it stays in place. Can you find out the name of the Roman version of the messenger god?

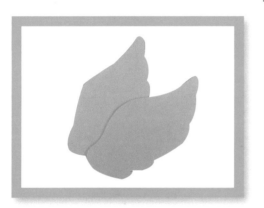

1 For each pair of wings, cut out two wing shapes from stiff, white card.

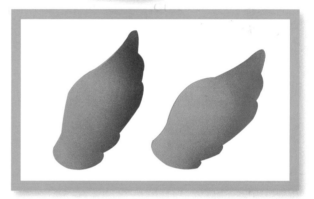

2 Use gold spray paint on the edges of the wings. Leave to dry.

! Ask an adult to use the spray paint.

3 Attach fluffy white feathers to the wings with PVA glue. Leave to dry.

4 Glue the wings a few centimetres apart on a piece of gold ribbon.

GLOSSARY

aristocrat a member of a rich, land-owning family

bronze metal made from copper and tin

candidate a person who puts themselves forward for a post or honour

chariot a light, two-wheeled vehicle, usually pulled by horses

circumference the distance around a shape, especially a circle

civilisation a society that is very advanced in science, technology, the arts, government and law

climate the weather a place experiences over a long period of time

colonies settlements established abroad by ancient Greeks who left their homes because of overcrowding and political problems

conquer to defeat an enemy or army and take over its lands

diameter a straight line running through the middle of a circle

discus a circular stone or metal plate used in throwing competitions

displace something or someone moved out of place, often by force

era a long period of history

gorgon a female monster in Greek mythology who had snakes for hair and could turn people to stone

government a group of people who run a country and make laws

immortal live forever

judge a person who is in charge of cases in a court of law

jury a group of people who decide if a person is guilty or innocent in a court of law

kiln a large oven for baking pottery

memorial something that remembers a dead person or past event

mythical not based in historical fact but dealing with supernatural characters, such as gods and heroes

Persia the modern country of Iran

philosophy in ancient Greece, philosophy meant 'knowledge'

prisoner of war a person captured by an enemy during a war

replica an exact copy of something, usually on a smaller scale

Romans a huge civilisation that ruled lands from Africa to Europe in 753 BCE–CE 476

symbolise to represent something or stand for something else

truce an agreement to stop fighting for a time

tunic a hip-length or knee-length garment

BOOKS

It's All About ... Glorious Greeks by Charles Taylor (Kingfisher)
Greek Gazette (Newspaper Histories) by Fergus Flemming (Usborne)
At Home With: The Ancient Greeks by Tim Cooke (Wayland)
Horrible Histories: Groovy Greeks by Terry Deary (Scholastic)
History Showtime: Ancient Greeks by Liza Phipps and Avril Thompson (Franklin Watts)

PLACES TO VISIT

Greek objects, art and buildings can be seen in many museums, including these listed below. If you can't visit, check out their websites for lots of interesting information.

British Museum (London, England)
National Archaeological Museum (Athens, Greece)
Antikensammlung (Berlin, Germany)

Herakleion Archaeological Museum (Crete, Greece)
The Acropolis Museum (Athens, Greece)

WEBSITES

A BBC website about the ancient Greeks:
www.bbc.co.uk/education/topics/z87tn39

Two British Museum websites explore ancient Greece using hundreds of objects and resources from the museum's collection:
www.ancientgreece.co.uk
www.britishmuseum.org/learning/schools_and_teachers/resources/cultures/ancient_greece.aspx

A National Geographic website with ten fascinating facts:
www.ngkids.co.uk/history/10-facts-about-the-ancient-greeks

NOTE TO PARENTS AND TEACHERS:

Every effort has been made by the Publishers to ensure that these websites are suitable for children, that they are of the highest educational value, and that they contain no inappropriate or offensive material. However, because of the nature of the Internet, it is impossible to guarantee that the contents of these sites will not be altered. We strongly advise that Internet access is supervised by a responsible adult.

INDEX

QUIZ ANSWERS

Page 5.   b – Minotaur. The Minotaur was a beast with the head of a bull and the body of a man.

Page 7.   a – red. Experts believe Spartan men were given a new red cloak every year.

Page 12.   c – a building. Tholos were circular in shape.

Page 14.   b – stone tokens.

Page 20.   c – to scare the enemy.

Page 22.   b – In a large pot! He believed in living a life of poverty. He begged for a living and slept in a large ceramic pot in a marketplace!

Page 27.   a – a coin.